SUPER SIMPLE
EARTH INVESTIGATIONS

SUPER SIMPLE
ROCK CYCLE
PROJECTS

Science Activities for
Future Petrologists

JESSIE ALKIRE

CONSULTING EDITOR, DIANE CRAIG, M.A./READING SPECIALIST

Super Sandcastle

An Imprint of Abdo Publishing
abdopublishing.com

abdopublishing.com

Published by Abdo Publishing, a division of ABDO, PO Box 398166, Minneapolis, Minnesota 55439. Copyright © 2018 by Abdo Consulting Group, Inc. International copyrights reserved in all countries. No part of this book may be reproduced in any form without written permission from the publisher. Super SandCastle™ is a trademark and logo of Abdo Publishing.

Printed in the United States of America, North Mankato, Minnesota
102017
012018

Design: Kelly Doudna, Mighty Media, Inc.
Production: Mighty Media, Inc.
Editor: Liz Salzmann
Cover Photographs: Mighty Media, Inc.; Shutterstock
Interior Photographs: Mighty Media, Inc.; Science Source; Shutterstock; Wikimedia Commons

The following manufacturers/names appearing in this book are trademarks: Essential Everyday®, Morton®, Pyrex®, Westcott™

Publisher's Cataloging-in-Publication Data

Names: Alkire, Jessie, author.
Title: Super simple rock cycle projects: science activities for future petrologists / by Jessie Alkire.
Other titles: Science activities for future petrologists
Description: Minneapolis, Minnesota : Abdo Publishing, 2018. | Series: Super simple earth investigations
Identifiers: LCCN 2017946519 | ISBN 9781532112393 (lib.bdg.) | ISBN 9781614799818 (ebook)
Subjects: LCSH: Petrology--Juvenile literature. | Geochemical cycles--Juvenile literature. | Science--Experiments--Juvenile literature.
Classification: DDC 507.8--dc23
LC record available at https://lccn.loc.gov/2017946519

TO ADULT HELPERS

The projects in this title are fun and simple. There are just a few things to remember to keep kids safe. Some projects require the use of sharp or hot objects. Also, kids may be using messy materials such as glue or paint. Make sure they protect their clothes and work surfaces. Review the projects before starting, and be ready to assist when necessary.

KEY SYMBOLS

Watch for these warning symbols in this book. Here is what they mean.

HOT!
You will be working with something hot. Get help!

SHARP!
You will be working with a sharp object. Get help!

CONTENTS

WHAT IS THE ROCK CYCLE?

The rock cycle is a **geological** process. It is how rocks are formed. Rocks are also changed and destroyed in the cycle. Each kind of rock can become another kind over and over again.

CRUMBLING ROCKS

Most of Earth's crust is made up of rocks. They can be found underground and on Earth's surface. Rocks also shape **landforms** around us.

Rocks are made of **minerals**. Some are made of one mineral. Others are made of many minerals. Rocks can be many shapes, colors, and sizes.

STONE FENCE

Rocks are important. They have had many purposes throughout history. Their uses include tools, weapons, and building supplies. **Minerals** from rocks are used to create chemicals and other **substances** we need.

STONE ARROWHEADS

TYPES OF ROCKS

Three kinds of rocks make up the rock cycle. Each kind can become one of the other kinds through the rock cycle.

IGNEOUS ROCKS

Igneous rocks form from **magma**. Magma cools and hardens into igneous rocks. These rocks can be formed underground. They can also be formed above ground after a **volcano** erupts. Granite is a type of igneous rock.

SEDIMENTARY ROCKS

Erosion helps form sedimentary rocks. Wind and water **erode** rocks. The rocks break into pieces called sediments. The sediments pile up in layers. Pressure pushes the layers together. This creates sedimentary rocks. Sandstone is a type of sedimentary rock.

METAMORPHIC ROCKS

Metamorphic rocks start underground as other kinds of rocks. The rocks change due to heat and pressure within Earth. This creates metamorphic rocks. Marble is a type of metamorphic rock.

HOW SCIENTISTS STUDY THE ROCK CYCLE

Some scientists study the rock cycle. They are called petrologists. There are three main branches of petrology. Each branch studies one kind of rock.

Petrologists travel the world. They collect rock samples. Then they study the rocks in labs.

Scientists use special microscopes to study rocks up close. They look at a rock's structure. They do tests to find out what **minerals** the rock is made of. They try to find out how the rock formed. Then they **classify** the rock.

A PETROLOGIST IN THE LAB

JAMES HUTTON

James Hutton was a **geologist**. He was born in Scotland in 1726. Hutton studied law and medicine before becoming a farmer. He then started studying rocks. Hutton came up with the idea of a rock cycle. At the time, people believed Earth was 6,000 years old. Hutton proved it was much older.

Studying rocks is important. Rocks teach us about Earth's history. They tell us what **minerals** are found below Earth's surface. They give clues about other geological processes.

THE GRAND CANYON

EXPOSED ROCK LAYERS

MATERIALS

Here are some of the materials that you will need for the projects in this book.

ALUMINUM FOIL **BOUILLON CUBES** **BOWLS** **CRAYONS** **DINNER KNIFE** **EGGS & EGG CARTON**

FOOD COLORING **GRAVEL** **LARGE CLEAR JAR WITH LID** **LIQUID MEASURING CUP** **MARBLES** **MOSS**

NAIL

NOTEBOOK

PAPER CUPS

PAPER PLATE

PAPER TOWELS

PITCHER

PLASTIC BAGS

PLASTIC BIN

PLASTIC BOTTLES

SALT

SAND

SUGAR CUBES

TIPS AND TECHNIQUES

The best way to learn about rocks is to study them! You can gather rocks from outside or buy a rock kit. You can look at rocks up close with a magnifying glass. You can write down a rock's qualities. These include its color, its size, how it feels, and more.

CRAYON ROCK CYCLE

MATERIALS: crayons in several colors, paper plate, dinner knife, aluminum foil, plastic bag, bowl, hot water

Rocks are formed, changed, and destroyed in the rock cycle. There are igneous, sedimentary, and metamorphic rocks. Changes occur due to the amount of heat and pressure on the rocks.

1 Remove the crayons' wrappers.

2 Use a dinner knife to scrape the crayons into tiny pieces. Put each color on a different paper plate.

3 Sprinkle a layer of each color of crayon on a small piece of aluminum foil.

4 Place another piece of foil on top of the crayon pieces.

Continued on the next page.

5 Press down firmly with your hands.

6 Lift the top piece of foil. **Examine** your crayon rock. The pressure formed a sedimentary rock!

7 Place the sedimentary rock in a plastic bag.

8 Have an adult help you heat a bowl of water in the microwave.

9 Dip the plastic bag in the hot water. Leave it there just until the crayon pieces start to melt.

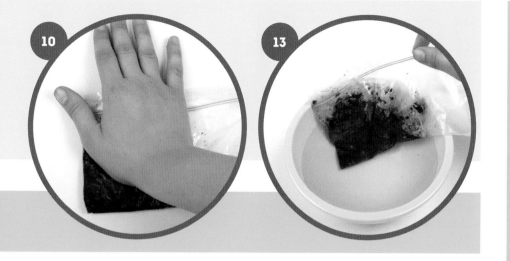

10 Let the bag cool just until it is safe to touch. Press on the bag to flatten it.

11 Carefully remove the rock from the bag. **Examine** it. The heat and pressure formed a metamorphic rock!

12 Put the metamorphic rock back in the bag.

13 Place the bag in hot water until the crayon pieces are completely melted. Remove the bag from the water.

14 Let the crayon cool completely before removing it from the bag.

15 Examine your rock. The **extreme** heat and cooling formed an igneous rock!

DIGGING DEEPER

The whole crayons represent igneous rocks formed from **magma**.

Scraping the rocks is **erosion** wearing away the rock. Your hand is the pressure that creates layers of sedimentary rock.

Then, the hot water and pressure of your hand is the heat and pressure underground as more layers of rock pile up. This creates metamorphic rock.

Finally, leaving the crayon in the water until it melts is like the extreme heat below Earth's crust. It melts the rock into magma. When the magma cools, it forms new igneous rock!

SAND EROSION MODEL

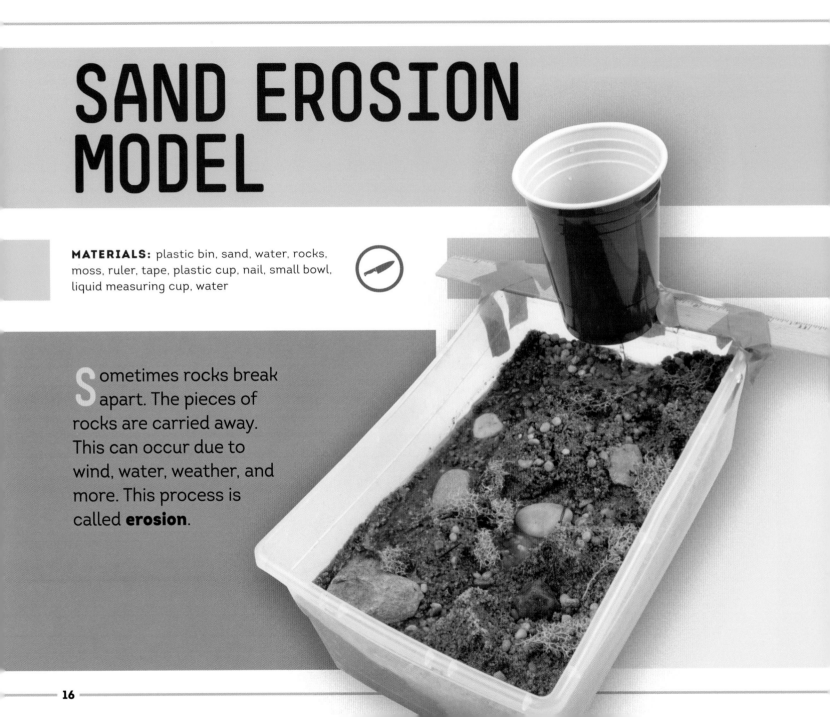

MATERIALS: plastic bin, sand, water, rocks, moss, ruler, tape, plastic cup, nail, small bowl, liquid measuring cup, water

Sometimes rocks break apart. The pieces of rocks are carried away. This can occur due to wind, water, weather, and more. This process is called **erosion**.

① Fill a plastic bin halfway with sand. Add enough water so the sand sticks together.

② Use your hands to create **landforms** in the sand. Make hills, cliffs, valleys, and more. Some should be tightly packed. Make others loosely packed.

③ Place rocks in the bin. Press some rocks into the sides of landforms.

④ Press moss into the sides of some of your landforms.

⑤ Sprinkle small rocks and moss throughout the bin.

⑥ Tape a ruler across one end of the bin.

Continued on the next page.

7 Use a nail to make a hole in the bottom of the cup.

8 Tape the cup to the ruler. Make sure the hole in the cup isn't over the ruler.

9 Put a small bowl under the ruler end of the bin.

10 Pour water into the cup. Water should drip out of the hole in the cup. Keep pouring!

11 Watch the water's path. How does it affect the sand **landforms**? This is **erosion** at work!

Water is a common cause of **erosion**. Rain, rivers, and other water sources flow over the ground. The force of the water can break and shape **landforms** and rocks over time. The water also carries rocks, sediments, and other matter as it moves. These **substances** are dropped by the water as it slows down.

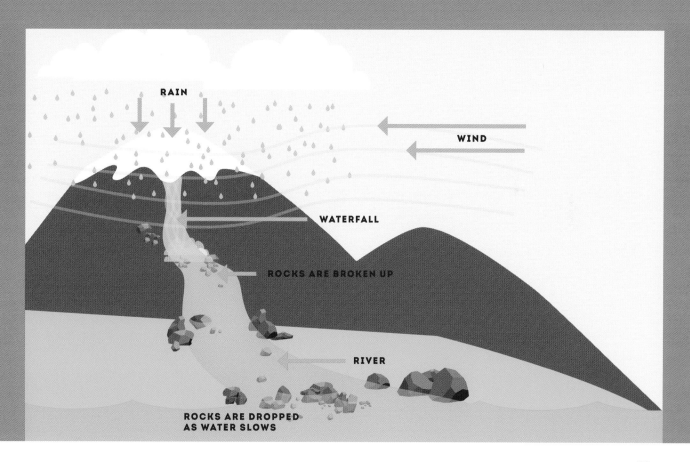

RAIN

WIND

WATERFALL

ROCKS ARE BROKEN UP

RIVER

ROCKS ARE DROPPED
AS WATER SLOWS

SEDIMENT JAR

MATERIALS: large clear jar with lid, soil, rocks, sand, pitcher, water, pencil, notebook

Water carries rocks, sediments, and other matter to new locations. As the water slows, these **substances** start to settle. This process is called deposition.

① Add soil, rocks, and sand to the jar. Fill it halfway.

② Add water to the jar until it is almost full.

③ Place a lid on the jar. Make sure it is on tight!

④ Shake the jar.

⑤ Leave the jar for at least one day.

⑥ Observe how the contents of the jar have settled. How many layers are there? Write down your findings!

WEATHERING CUBES

MATERIALS: 2 marbles, bouillon cube, sugar cube, 2 empty plastic bottles, timer, plate

Weathering is when rocks break down and wear away. This can be caused by plants, animals, wind, water, and more. Weathering affects some rocks more than others.

1 Place a marble and a bouillon cube in a plastic bottle.

2 Place a marble and sugar cube in the other plastic bottle.

3 Put the caps on both bottles.

4 Shake the bottles at the same time for one minute. This represents weathering.

5 Carefully empty the bottles onto a plate. Remove the marbles from the plate.

6 Observe how the cubes have changed. Which one was changed most by the weathering?

ROCK IN A CUP

MATERIALS: 2 paper cups, spoon, sand, gravel, water, sugar, plastic plate, magnifying glass (optional)

Some rocks are made of pieces of other rocks. Rocks break apart due to weathering and **erosion**. The pieces are pressed together to form a new sedimentary rock.

1 Put a spoonful of gravel in a paper cup.

2 Add a spoonful of sand. Stir the gravel and sand together.

3 Pour a spoonful of water into the second paper cup.

4 Add five spoonfuls of sugar to the second paper cup. Stir well.

5 Pour the sugar mixture into the sand and gravel mixture. Stir well.

6 Set the cup aside and let the rock dry.

7 Once the rock is dry, turn the cup upside down on a plate so the rock comes out.

8 **Examine** your sedimentary rock. You can look at it up close with a magnifying glass!

SPARKLING EGGSHELL GEODES

MATERIALS: eggs, bowls, liquid measuring cup, water, paper towel, egg carton, salt, spoon, 3–4 small cups, food coloring

A geode is a hollow rock with crystals inside. Sometimes rocks have empty space inside them. Crystals grow in the space. This forms a geode.

1 Carefully crack the eggs into a bowl. You only need the shells for the project.

2 Gently rinse and dry the eggshells. Try not to break them!

3 Place the eggshells in an egg carton.

4 Have an adult help you boil about 3 cups of water. Carefully pour the boiling water into a bowl.

5 Add salt to the water. Stir well. Keep adding salt until no more will **dissolve**.

Continued on the next page.

6 Pour the salt water into a liquid measuring cup.

7 Divide the salt water evenly between the small cups.

8 Add food coloring to each cup. Use any colors you'd like!

9 Fill the eggshells with the different colors of salt water. Set the egg carton in a safe place out of the way.

10 Observe the crystals each day as they start to form. It should take about a week for the crystals to fully grow.

DIGGING DEEPER

Igneous rocks can have spaces inside them. The spaces are created by air bubbles in **magma**. When the magma cools, the air bubbles leave spaces. Groundwater flows through the spaces. The water has **minerals** in it. The minerals grow crystals that fill the spaces. This takes thousands of years!

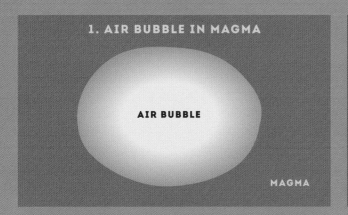

1. AIR BUBBLE IN MAGMA

AIR BUBBLE

MAGMA

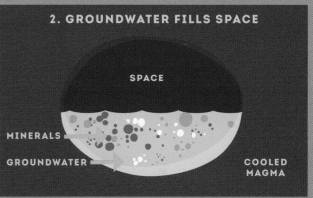

2. GROUNDWATER FILLS SPACE

SPACE

MINERALS

GROUNDWATER

COOLED MAGMA

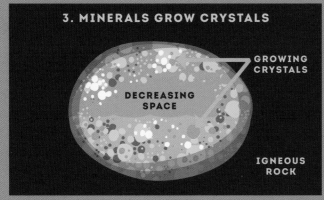

3. MINERALS GROW CRYSTALS

GROWING CRYSTALS

DECREASING SPACE

IGNEOUS ROCK

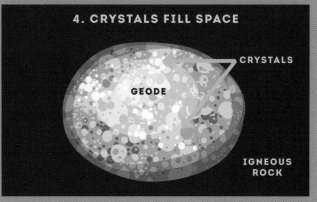

4. CRYSTALS FILL SPACE

CRYSTALS

GEODE

IGNEOUS ROCK

CONCLUSION

The rock cycle is a **geological** process. Rocks are formed, changed, and destroyed in the cycle. Petrologists study rocks and the rock cycle. They learn about Earth's history and its processes!

QUIZ

1. What are rocks made of?

2. Igneous rocks form from **magma**.
   TRUE OR FALSE?

3. How old did people think Earth was when James Hutton lived?

LEARN MORE ABOUT IT!

You can find out more about the rock cycle at the library. Or you can ask an adult to help you **research** the rock cycle **online**!

Answers: 1. Minerals 2. True 3. 6,000 years

GLOSSARY

classify – to put things in groups according to their characteristics.

dissolve – to become part of a liquid.

erode – to wear away, especially by wind or water. This process is erosion.

examine – to look at closely.

extreme – very much, or to a very great degree.

geological – related to the science of Earth's structure, such as rocks and layers of soil. Someone who studies this type of science is a geologist.

landform – a natural feature of Earth's surface, such as a mountain or valley.

magma – melted rock below Earth's surface.

mineral – a chemical element or compound that occurs naturally in the ground.

online – connected to the Internet.

research – to find out more about something.

substance – anything that takes up space, such as a solid object or a liquid.

volcano – a deep hole in Earth's surface that magma comes out of.